UNIT 731

THE FORGOTTEN AUSCHWITZ

SECOND EDITION

BY DEREK PUA

DANIELLE DYBBRO AND ALISTAIR ROGERS

TABLE OF CONTENTS

Preface 5

Introduction 7

Chapter 1: Beginnings 9

Chapter 2: Duties Of 731 23

Chapter 3: Use Of Humans As Test Subjects 29

Chapter 4: Other Experiments 35

Chapter 5: Deployment Of Biological And Chemical
Weapons 43

Chapter 6: The Fall 53

Chapter 7: Post-War "Legacy" 57

Chapter 8: Post-War Denial 69

Conclusion 79

References 83

SECOND EDITION
FOREWORD

I vaguely remember learning about Japanese war crimes in school, but Unit 731 was something that I had never heard of in my life. I started doing some precursory research and read about human experiments done in the name of advancing the medical field, or simply for the satisfaction of scientific curiosity. This sounded similar to the experiments conducted by the Nazis during World War II; however, while the Nazi narrative is well-versed in school curriculums, Asian victims who were affected by Japanese imperial oppression and military aggression are largely left out of the historical discussion in education.

As I started reading about the experiments, at first I was horrified, but I was soon numbed to the descriptions, of civilians that were cut open without anesthetic after being deliberately infected with the plague. I soon realized that the historical controversy surrounding Unit 731 is not so much what occurred during the experiments themselves, but rather the more than 70 years of insufficient apologies and, at times, denial of Japan's systematic and militarily sanctioned biological warfare research program.

For me personally, this research has allowed me to dig deeper into the Pacific theater of World War II through the lens of Japan and China, rather than the European and American narrative focus that I know well.

Through the research done for this second edition, I hope that others not only can learn something new about the experience of World War II, but can learn to think critically about issues from this time period.

The call for the Japanese government to fully apologize for the crimes committed at Unit 731, and other facilities, has joined similar demands for international recognition of the countless victims of Japanese imperial control. However, important to note is that the Japanese government is not isolated in debating the legitimacy of claims of Japanese war crimes victims. The government documents and trial transcripts I examined reveal inconsistencies from both the Japanese and the American governments that, frankly, are unnerving.

– Danielle Dybbro, 2017

PREFACE

Growing up in Hong Kong, I heard much about the terrors that my grandparents on both sides of the family had endured under the rule of the Japanese during their invasions of Pacific East Asia. One grandfather narrowly escaped with his life during the bombing of Shanghai and another was recruited as a child soldier in British Malaya. While these tales horrified me as a child, it sparked an interest in me that would set me on the path of attaining my bachelor's degree in history at the University of San Francisco. I was so intrigued by the subject that by the time I was fourteen, I had read Iris Chang's award winning book, *The Rape of Nanking: The Forgotten Holocaust of World War II,* which was a gift from my grandfather, who insisted that this portion of history can never be forgotten. I took these words to heart and made it my mission to ensure just that.

I was first introduced to the topic of Japan's biological weapon program when I was just 15 years old during a family vacation to Harbin in Heilongjiang province. Although it has been a long time since then, I clearly remember the shock and dread that befell me as I made my way through the ruins of Unit 731. By this point, I had already known much about Japanese war crimes that were carried out during the war, but Unit 731 was much different; my research has introduced me to a whole new level of brutality that I previously thought was unfathomable. How one can commit such inhumane acts on his fellow man I will never know.

The topic of Unit 731 eluded my curiosity for much of my childhood despite my personal attachment to the subject of Japanese war crimes, and wouldn't enter into my scope of research until my first year of university. By that point, I had researched multiple atrocities committed by the Japanese during the Second World War, but Japan's biological weapons program exceeds all of them in its brutality and inhumanity.

As I grew up, I realized that most people in the world, even my peers in Hong Kong, were either indifferent or ignorant of the subject. Though I was disappointed by this realization, it continues to provide me with the motivation and drive to spread the knowledge of this largely forgotten past; as the age-old expression by George Santayana goes: "*Those who forget history are condemned to repeat it.*"

– Derek Pua, 2016

INTRODUCTION

Unit 731 was the main administrative hub in a network of research facilities under Imperial Japan's top secret biological weapons program. The program was headed by Major General Shiro Ishii. Ishii and his team performed innumerable inhumane experiments on Chinese, Russian, and American prisoners. These prisoners were dehumanized and referred to as "marutas," or logs. Some prisoners were infected with diseases, then vivisected after a period of time to observe the disease's effect on human anatomy. Some were used to test the effective ranges of bombs and certain weapons, while others were forced to endure excruciating frostbite experiments. These are only a few examples of the experiments carried out by the Japanese.

One could argue that these Japanese atrocities carried out were typical of the chaos and brutality that often accompany warfare; but this cannot be said for Unit 731. Much like their counterparts in Nazi Germany did in the Auschwitz Concentration Camp, the Japanese experimented on humans like lab rats, all in the name of medical and military advancement.

The full extent of Unit 731's experiments is not known, but since the 1980s more information has emerged due to admissions of guilt from former members, testimonies from soldiers civilians, the declassifying of government documents, and the unearthing of previously unknown sources. As the scholarship continues to evolve, it is important to understand that for East Asia, the American declaration of war against Japan at the end of 1941 came over a decade after Japan's invasion and occupation of Manchuria. And with the establishment of the puppet state of Manchukuo, the implementation of Japan's secret biological warfare research was soon to follow.

CHAPTER 1

Beginnings

The Early Life of Shiro Ishii

Japan's involvement with biological warfare begins and ends with one man: Shiro Ishii. Ishii had a long interest in biological warfare and understanding the limits of what the human body could endure under very harsh conditions and treatments. Despite an intellect that was apparent to his superiors, Ishii had rightfully developed the reputation as a heartless, sadistic individual, who cared little for the suffering he imposed on his victims. A closer look into his life before becoming the head of Unit 731 helps present a clearer understanding of his desire to advance Japan's biological and chemical warfare program in the Far East during the Asia-Pacific War of 1931-1945.

Shiro Ishii was born June 25th, 1892, in the village of Chiyoda, south of the capital of Tokyo. He was the fourth son of a relatively wealthy family that reigned over the local community in a feudal manner despite the abolition of feudalism that came with the Meiji Restoration nearly 30 years before[1]. Specific ideas that did come with Meiji Restoration were rapid advancements in industrialization, nationalism, and expansion as an international power. Loyalty to the Emperor became a central tenet to Japan's national identity; democratic values were introduced to the country with limited suffrage and a representative body (the Diet); and the military was rebuilt on Western ideas, which contributed to major military victories over China (1895) and Russia (1905). The Japan of the late 19th and early 20th Century was the perfect setting for a man of Shiro's capabilities to rise professionally and make a career for himself. It also shaped his world perspective, which included belief in the supremacy of Japan over other nations and an undying loyalty to the Emperor.

Not much is known about Ishii's childhood, although considering he was the fourth son in a relatively wealthy family, it is safe to assume he attended primary and secondary schools[2]. His teachers realized he was a gifted student with much potential. While he was naturally interested in medicine, Shiro also wanted to act

---

[1] Gold, Hal. *Unit 731, Testimony.*

[2] Byrd, Gregory Dean "General Ishii Shiro: His Legacy is That of Genius and Madman." Masters Thesis, East Tennessee State University, 2005. 15.

on his nationalistic bend and serve in the Japanese Imperial Army. He combined these two passions to set himself on the path to becoming a medical doctor in the Japanese Imperial Army, and was accepted into the Medical Department of Kyoto International University in 1916.

While his talents and ability were well known among his professors and university administration, he was not very popular with his fellow students. Ishii took every advantage to gain proximity to his superiors and the academic administration in order to advance his career. He also made a habit of using lab equipment that was cleaned and organized by his fellow students during the evening without taking the time to clean it himself after conducting his own research.[3] Medical ethics were also not widely discussed at the University, nor was a Hippocratic Oath administered. This paved the way for Shiro to view his subjects as test fodder and not patients whose well-being he was in charge of. Regardless of such shortcomings, Shiro graduated from the Medical Department from Kyoto Imperial University in 1920.[4]

Ishii entered the army one month later and began his military training and after his basic training

[3] Byrd, 16.
[4] Harris, Sheldon. *Factories of Death: Japanese biological warfare 1932-45 and the American cover-up.* 14-15.

and a number of transfers, was stationed at the First Army Hospital in 1922 in Tokyo. While at the capital, he engaged in behavior not entirely becoming a respected student from a wealthy family. Shiro partook in womanizing and heavy bouts of drinking throughout Tokyo's red light district. He was known to seek the services of very young geisha girls, and carry on throughout that neighborhood intoxicated. In spite of such distractions, Ishii was recommended for postgraduate studies, and returned to Kyoto Imperial University, eventually earning his PhD in 1927[5].

That same year, Ishii read an article on the 1925 Geneva Convention outlawing biological and chemical warfare. In the age of internationalism and collective security, the prohibition of biological and chemical weapons was viewed as a step to preventing the indiscriminate harm and destruction of the First World War. While the Japanese delegation to the convention signed the agreement, it was not ratified by the Diet[6]; therefore, Japan was not bound to that agreement, and had the freedom to develop a chemical and biological weapons program. In this global desire to ban such weapons, Ishii saw an opportunity, believing that if the entire world was willing to outlaw such a weapon, it

---

[5] Harris, 16-17.
[6] Byrd, 16.

could pose benefits for a Japanese nation desiring expansion throughout the Far East.

With the blessing of both his superiors in both the army and navy, Ishii began research into the theoretical uses of biological and chemical warfare, promoting the argument that producing bacteria would be less expensive than other conventional forms of weaponry. In the spring of 1928, he travelled extensively abroad, visiting numerous European countries and gathered research on biological warfare, some of which came from the US, Germany, Russia, France, and Italy, as well as Switzerland, Turkey, the Soviet Union, Egypt, Singapore, Ceylon, and Canada[7]. While some countries were engaged in the secret development of biological weaponry, his trip did not yield a great amount of information or research.

Ishii returned in 1930 to a more nationalistic Japan that desired expansion and supremacy throughout the Far East. The country's new slogan - a wealthy country, a strong army- was highly prevalent on the eve of the invasion of Manchuria. According to a secondary source, when Ishii finally returned to Japan from his world tour, he convinced the Japanese State Department

---

[7] Naito, Ryoichi. "The Naito Document: Private (Secret) Information to Colonel Sanders." 1945. Printed in Williams & Wallace; Harris, 19.

of Military Affairs that there was great potential in developing a biological weapons program, despite possible international condemnation.[8]

Although the use of chemical and biological warfare had been banned in the Geneva Convention of 1925, some countries were covertly researching bioweapons, as a Military Attaché in the Japanese Embassy in Washington D.C. "said that he heard that Ishii had studied bacteriological warfare at the Massachusetts Institute of Technology in Boston."[9]

However, in a primary source testimony from the Khabarovsk War Crime Trials conducted by the Soviets, a former Unit 731 member claimed that in a meeting in 1941, Ishii explained the reason for Japan's interest in biological warfare. Ishii said this was because "Japan did not possess sufficient natural resources of metals and other raw materials required for the manufacture of weapons," which meant that Japan "had to develop new types of weapons" and that "all the great powers were carrying on corresponding work in [the

---

[8] Global Alliance for Preserving the History of WWII in Asia. *The Story of Unit 731*. (2008), 2.
[9] Tsuneishi & Asano, *Suicide of Two Physicians*, 48. Quoted in Harris, Sheldon. *Factories of Death: Japanese biological warfare 1932-45 and the American cover-up*, 19.

sphere of bacteriological warfare] and that Japan must not lag behind in this field."[10]

Dr. Shiro Ishii[11]

The beginnings of Unit 731

Ishii's opportunity to explore the potentials of biological warfare came with the invasion of Manchuria in 1931. The landscape of Manchuria itself, with wide expanses of rural, uninhabited land, was the perfect setting for Ishii

---

[10] Yamada, Otozo. *Materials on the trial of former servicemen of the Japanese Army, charged with manufacturing and employing bacteriological weapon.* Moscow: Foreign Languages Pub. House, 1950. Accessed via Google Books. 113-114. Testimony of Kawashima.
[11] Takezawa Masao. *Shiro Ishii.1932.* In *Bulletin of Unit 731.* *https://commons.wikimedia.org/wiki/File:Shiro-ishii.jpg*

to conduct his research away from the cramped, limited space of the island of Japan.

Within the first two years of Japanese imperial control of Manchuria, Ishii established research facilities there, both for defensive and offensive biological warfare. Defensive research was the production of vaccines and offensive research was for mobilizing diseases as weapons, including plague, glanders, and anthrax among others. By the time the Western powers had initiated World War II in 1939, historians estimate there were at least 18 biological warfare facilities established throughout the Japanese empire, located as far north as Manchuria and as far south as Indonesia.[12]

The Japanese Army's first germ research facility was built in the town of Beiyinhe, outside of Harbin in Manchuria, and was also known as the Zhong Ma Prison Camp.[13] In 1932 the village was evacuated and taken over by Ishii and his colleagues, and the initial research was focused on anthrax, glanders, and plague, and

---

[12] Pawlowicz, Rachel and Grunden, Walter. "Teaching Atrocities: The Holocaust and Unit 731 in Secondary School Curriculum." *History Teacher*, Vol. 48 Issue 2, p. 271-294, February 2015. 274-6.
[13] Federation of American Scientists. "Biological Weapons Program." 2000. Accessed via Alpha Education online resources.

included live dissections of prisoners.[14] Other experiments served as precursors of the Unit 731 experiments, including the testing of poison gas, high voltage tolerance, poison injections, frostbite remedies, and the removal of organs for further research while the prisoner was still alive.[15]

The prisoners that were used in the experiments were mostly Chinese, but Soviets, Mongolians, and Koreans that were arrested by the Japanese army were also used. The prisoners were those that were arrested as spies and resisters to the Japanese in Manchuria, and were scheduled to be executed without a trial, so using them for experiments was deemed a better use of their lives than merely executing them.[16] In fact, some of the medical officials working at the research facilities were fully aware that the subjects brought for research "were [already] doomed to die."[17] After the prisoners died

---

[14] Harris, Sheldon, *Factories of Death: Japanese Biological Warfare, 1932-45, and the American Cover-up* (New York: Routledge 2007). 25.

[15] Harris, 28.

[16] Tsuchiya, Takashi. "The Imperial Japanese Medical Atrocities and its Enduring Legacy in Japanese Research Ethics." Abridged from chapter "The Imperial Japanese Experiments in China" in *Oxford Textbook of Clinical Research Ethics*, 2008.

[17] Yamada, Otozo. *Materials on the trial of former servicemen of the Japanese Army, charged with manufacturing and employing*

from experimentation, their bodies were gotten rid of by way of an electric furnace.[18] The Zhong Ma Camp was eventually destroyed and the program was transferred to two newly set up research facilities: one near the city of Changchun and the other one in the Pingfan district, just south of Harbin.

Unit 100

The Anti-Epizootic Protection of Horses Unit in Changchun was later renamed as Unit 100. It was not headed by Ishii, but rather was controlled by a veterinarian, Major Yujiro, who would partake in joint research with Ishii. The special focus of Unit 100 was animal disease prevention, but the facility also participated in plant and animal biological warfare experiments. Unit 100's research on crop viruses and livestock diseases was intended for future sabotage operations against their enemies.

    The facility was staffed by veterinarians, microbiologists, chemists, and agriculturalists, with the capability of mass-producing large amounts of anthrax, glanders, sheep and cattle herd plagues, as well as red

---

bacteriological weapon. Moscow: Foreign Languages Pub. House, 1950. 325.

[18] Grunden, Walter E. *Secret Weapons and World War II: Japan in the shadow of big science.* Lawrence, Kansas: University Press of Kansas, 2005. 186.

rust. Field tests conducted along the Soviet-Manchurian border region began as early as 1941.[19] The unit's leaders hoped that in the event of a Soviet invasion of Manchuria, infected animals coming from Unit 100 would be dispersed and start epidemics among the nearby Soviet livestock.[20] According to a number of testimonies from Harris, former workers and medical students witnessed both humans and animals as victims of experimentation. They saw dead bodies wheeled away from operating rooms and animals being poisoned with contaminated food.[21]

Unit 731

The facility at Pingfan was called the Kwantung Army Water Supply and Epidemic Prevention Department, and would be renamed as the infamous Unit 731 in 1941.[22]Unit 731's main mission was to research and produce germ-based weapons in massive quantities for the Japanese Army. It took two years to construct the establishment's 150 buildings with a perimeter of 4 miles, which included living accommodations for its workers, a railway, an incinerator, a power supply, and

---

[19] Global Alliance, 5; 9.
[20] Global Alliance, 10.
[21] Harris, 87-90.
[22] Global Alliance, 2.

an airfield.[23] By 1940, there were 3,000 workers stationed at the facility.[24]

During Unit 731's lifetime, it is estimated that anywhere from 3,000 to 10,000 subjects were killed in medical experiments.[25] The subjects were mostly Han Chinese, but other groups that were killed included Russian Jews, Mongolians, Koreans, the mentally disabled, criminals, communist spies, and captured Allied soldiers.[26] Additionally, the low estimate of 3,000 only covers the period of 1941-1945, and does not include test subjects in Manchuria during the 1930s, subjects at nearby branch camps, other facilities not headed by Ishii (including Mukden and Changchun), or the unknown number of prisoners slaughtered following the Japanese surrender.[27]

---

[23] Reynolds, Gary. "U.S. Prisoners of War and Civilian American Citizens Captured and Interned by Japan in World War II: The Issue of Compensation," 18.

[24] Sanders. "The Sanders Report: Report on Scientific Intelligence Survey in Japan, September - October 1945." 1945. Printed in Williams & Wallace.

[25] Bix, Herbert P. *Hirohito and the Making of Modern Japan*. New York: HarperCollins, 2000. 617.

[26] Reynolds, 19. The ethnic makeup of the subjects is also listed in Harris, *Factories of Death*, 49.

[27] Harris, 66.

The map below includes the locations of major sites, also known as "death factories" for their high casualty rate. Major sites included Unit 9420 in Singapore, Unit 8604 in Guangdong (Canton), Unit 1644 in Nanjing (Nanking), Unit 1855 in Beijing, Unit 731 in Harbin, and Unit 100 in Changchun.

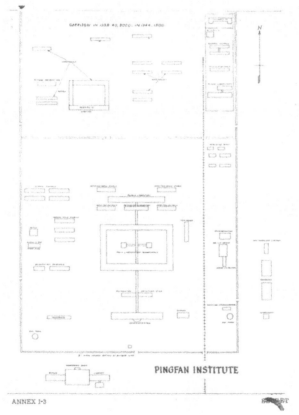

Hand Drawn map of Unit 731[28]

---

[28] Williams & Wallace.

21

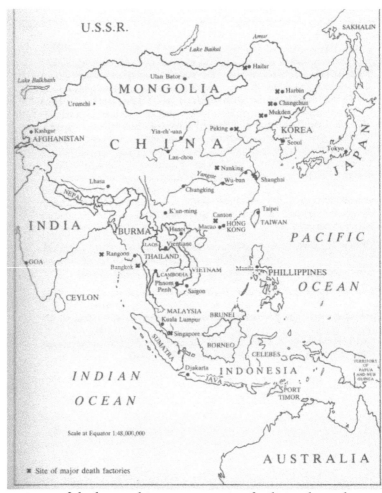

Some of the known bioweapon testing facilities throughout the Japanese Empire[29]

CHAPTER 2

Duties of 731

Unit 731 claimed to the public that its sole responsibility was the prevention of diseases and epidemics. In reality, it was a site for the research and preparation of biological and chemical warfare. Unit 731 and its sister facilities experimented with a wide variety of diseases such as the bubonic plague, anthrax, dysentery, typhoid, cholera, salmonella, and other diseases. The research obtained from these experiments led to the development of vaccines for the treatment of such diseases, as well as the manufacturing and deployment of chemical and biological weapons.

Unit 731 members who reported to the Ro Block, at the center of the facility, worked in the bacteria production and research laboratory. Workers in the Ro block were subjected to the putrid stench of rotting flesh and were constantly at risk of being exposed to the deadly diseases they experimented with. Cautionary

23

measures, including protective clothing, were taken. Researchers developed hand signals to communicate with one another while wearing protective gear; additionally, apples were used as a protection against infection. The workers believed that chewing and spitting out the slices of apple would "absorb any live bacteria that had entered their mouths."[30]

The *Ro* Block was also where many of the prisoners were housed. *Ro* Block looked like a square from the outside, but it hid two buildings from public view, which were the center of bacterial production and disease research. Many of the laborers that worked on the construction of Unit 731 became the first batch of research subjects for the Japanese scientists.[31]

Selection of Pathogens

In order to weaponize diseases such as the plague, Ishii's staff bred fleas and exposed them to rats infected with the plague and other pathogens. These fleas were then extracted and placed into ceramic bombs. In a testimony from the Khabarovsk Trials, a former worker of Unit 731 plead guilty to cultivating typhoid, dysentery, and

---

[30] Williams & Wallace, 22-3.
[31] Global Alliance, 3.

tuberculosis for the purpose of researching biological warfare.[32]

In the Khabarovsk War Crime Trials conducted in 1949, a former head of a division of Unit 731 confirmed that in their facility, rats were "infected by inoculating them with plague vaccine, and then the fleas were infected by these rats."[33]

A Chinese woman walks through the remains of Unit 731's rat breeding cages[34]

Mass production of Germs

[32] Yamada, 82. Testimony of Kikuchi Norimitsu.
[33] Yamada, Otozo. Materials on the trial of former servicemen of the Japanese Army, charged with manufacturing and employing bacteriological weapon (Moscow: Foreign Languages Pub. House 1950), 256. Testimony of Kawashima, December 25, 1949.
[34] McCurry, Justin, Digital image. 2006. In *Japanese veteran admits vivisection tests on PoWs*.
http://www.theguardian.com/world/2006/nov/27/secondworldwar.japan

There were over three thousand researchers and technicians involved in the day to day activities of Unit 731. Many of these scientists came from the most technologically advanced and prestigious Japanese universities of the time.

Ishii recruited doctors and medical students, including those from Kyoto Imperial University, his alma mater[35]

During the late 1930s, it is estimated that Unit 731 was capable of producing billions of bacteria microbes in a matter of days.[36] In fact, according to preliminary

---

[35]Parry, Richard. Digital image. 2011. In *Gruesome secret threatens to surface from city park.*
http://www.thetimes.co.uk/tto/news/world/asia/article2874151.ece;
Grunden, 188.
[36] Grunden, 188.

investigatory findings from the Khabarovsk Trials, the facility had the capacity to produce upwards of 30,000,000 billion microbes in a few days.[37]

Researching a Delivery System

Once he had determined which diseases were most effective to weaponize, Ishii only needed to develop a delivery system for his plague-infected fleas, which were often unleashed on remote villages to gauge their effectiveness. The methods of delivery included directly contaminating water supplies and the releasing of plague infected rats covered with fleas. Ishii also created "plague flea sprayers in the shape of fountain pens and walking sticks."[38] Chocolates and other candies filled with bacteria, such as anthrax, were distributed.[39] During the Khabarovsk Trials, a former member of Unit 731 recalled one instance where bread rolls and biscuits were baked with typhoid and salmonella, which were then given to Chinese civilians and saboteurs in order to cause an epidemic.[40] There were hundreds of bomb experiments performed on human test subjects, a notable example being the Anda Test Site.

---

[37] Yamada, 13.
[38] Williams & Wallace, 29.
[39] Yamada, 286. Testimony of Nishi Toshihide.
[40] Yamada, 442. Testimony of Furuichi.

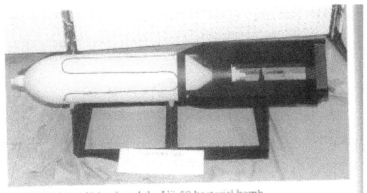

Ishii Shirō himself developed the Uji-50 bacterial bomb.

Shells packed with infected fleas were produced at Unit 731[41]

---

[41] Harris, Sheldon, *Factories of Death: Japanese Biological Warfare, 1932-45, and the American Cover-up.* 80-81.

CHAPTER 3

Use of Humans as Test Subjects

To determine the effectiveness of their weaponized diseases, Unit 731 and Unit 100 not only used livestock and other animals in their experiments, but also systematically used humans as guinea pigs in inhumane experiments. Live vivisections without the use of anesthesia were often performed to observe the effectiveness of pathogens.

Whilst the majority of test subjects were made up of ethnic Han Chinese, the Japanese also carried out experiments on captured Americans. American POWs liberated at Mukden POW camp testified that they had witnessed this or were themselves victims of similar medical experiments. In an interview, a former medical assistant at Unit 731 described the gruesome task of cutting open a person without the use of anesthetic:

> *"The fellow knew that it was over for him, and so he didn't struggle when they led him into the room and tied him down. But when I picked up the scalpel, that's when he*

began screaming. I cut him open from the chest to the stomach, and he screamed terribly, and his face was all twisted in agony. He made this unimaginable sound, he was screaming so horribly. But then finally he stopped. This was all in a day's work for the surgeons, but it really left an impression on me because it was my first time." [42]

The Term: *Maruta*

The term is loosely translated as "logs" in Japanese; it was a dehumanizing name, and test subjects were often regarded as subhuman. The dehumanization of the subjects served as a justification for the Japanese to conduct brutal experiments on them.

"We called the victims 'logs'... We didn't want to think of them as people. We didn't want to admit that we were taking lives. So we convinced ourselves that what we were doing was like cutting down a tree. When you see someone in that state, you just can't move. Your mind goes blank. The fear is overwhelming."

-Yoshio Shinuzaka [43]

---

[42] Kristof, Nicholas, "Unmasking Horror -- A special report,: Japan Confronting Gruesome War Atrocity," *New York Times* (Morioka, Japan), http://www.nytimes.com/1995/03/17/world/unmasking-horror-a-special-report-japan-confronting-gruesome-war-atrocity.html?pagewanted=all .

[43] Talmadge, Eric, "Japanese Soldier Faces the Poison of His Past," *Los Angeles Times*, September 19, 2004. http://articles.latimes.com/2004/sep/19/news/adfg-poison19/2

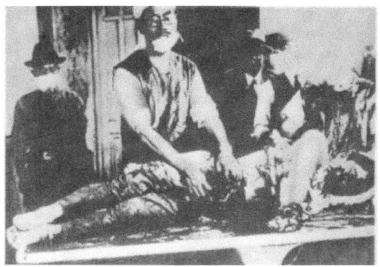

Ishii conducting autopsy on plague victim [44]

Unit 731 also had a Youth Corps consisting of 15-17 year old Japanese boys under its command. Members of the Corps received daily lessons in advanced subjects like mathematics, chemistry, biology, bacteriology, and linguistics. They also underwent harsh military training and were forced to assist with human experiments, as described by a former member of the youth corps:

> *"I had sprayed one Chinese with antiseptic, who had to be dissected dead or alive. His face was purple and blood oozed from it. Ooki the doctor ordered "two doses*

---

[44] Digital image. 1928. In 『山東省動乱記念写真帖』、昭和三年、青島新報 (1928). https://upload.wikimedia.org/wikipedia/commons/7/71/Autopsy_of_a_Japanese_victim_killed_in_the_Jinan_Incident.jpg.

of camphor". On the injection of camphor the Chinese opened his eyes, with tears and anger he stared blankly at the ceiling. Holding the Chinese's neck, Hoshijima used his hand to cut open the neck's vein with a knife. Due to pain and plague the Chinese fettered, Hoshijima pounded on his chest with the blunt of his knife and shouted "two doses of camphor" again, cutting open his vein. The Chinese shouted with a muted voice. "You son of a devil". Hoshijima cut from his upper abdomen to lower abdomen exposing his organs telling the effects of plague. The complete dissection took 20 minutes. The Chinese first lost his color and then his breath!"[45]

Sick and healthy patients were housed together to see how long it would take the healthy ones to get sick[46]

---

[45] Global Alliance, 18. Testimony from Tamura Yoshio, former member of Unit 731's Youth Corps.
[46] Global Alliance, 23.

32

The Anda Testing Site:

An open-air site, the Anda Testing Field, located 120 kilometers from Unit 731, was used to test the effectiveness of different kinds of bombs and explosives containing fleas and diseases, including plague and cholera. Bombs were dropped at different distances from subjects, and detailed notes were taken as the subjects experienced the symptoms and even died from the infections.[47] According to the Sanders Report, field tests with human subjects were conducted with the detonation of more than 2000 bombs.[48] One testimony in the Khabarovsk Trials also described the experimentation of gas gangrene bombs under subzero weather conditions, presumably to be used against the Soviets.[49]

The source of the "Marutas"

The term Maruta means wooden log, and was used to refer to the prisoners as a way to dehumanize them. Marutas were usually obtained from agencies and military police throughout Manchuria. Many of these test-subjects were communist party members and POWs

---

[47] Wilk, Beata Marzana. "The Japanese Biological and Chemical Warfare Program in China, 1932-1945." New Jersey: Masters Thesis, Seton Hall University, 2004. 32.
[48] Sanders Report.
[49] Yamada, 289. Testimony of Nishi Toshihide.

from China, Russia, and Mongolia. However, if the researchers ever needed more marutas, they would take civilians with the help of the *Kempeitai*. The closest source of prisoners to Unit 731 was a detention camp called Hogoin Camp, located 20 kilometers from PingFan. The camp's deputy chief, Kenji Yamagishi recalled that "during the entire period that [he] served at Hogoin camp, none of the prisoners dispatched [to Unit 731] ever returned."[50]

---

[50] Global Alliance,13.

CHAPTER 4

Other Experiments

The full extent of the experiments that Unit 731 and her sister facilities conducted is difficult to comprehend, not only because the nature of the experiments is disturbing to read and imagine, but also because official documentation is fragmented and hard to come by. Below are some examples based on testimonies from POWs and former medical workers that were witnesses to the experiments conducted in General Ishii's network of facilities that killed over an estimated 3,000 prisoners.[51]

Studies of Racial Differences on Immunity

Apart from the local population, there is evidence that more than 1,300 American troops were also sent to Mukden, a facility 350 miles from Unit 731 in Harbin,

---

[51] Bix, 617.

for experimentation.[52] They hoped to study racial differences from a "pathological point of view", and see how those of "Mongol origins" differed in their reactions from those of Anglo-Saxon origins. There is also evidence which indicates that survivors of the dreaded Bataan Death March were sent to Mukden for experimentation as well.[53] American and Allied prisoners of war were transported from the Philippines to Mukden on unmarked transport ships, aptly named "Hell Ships". It is estimated that at least 1,485 allied prisoners survived this arduous voyage only to be experimented on in these facilities.

"From the moment we went aboard that hell ship, they were experimenting on us. They threw us on board to see how much we could stand and many of us died. They took us from the tropics to a bitterly cold climate, and that took its toll on us. They gave us a few crackers and a little rice to eat and I feel that it was a systemic way of beginning to test us, to find out how much the Americans- and the British and Australians - could endure."

– Gregory Rodriguez, Senior [54]

---

[52] "Japanese Biological Warfare Experiments in World War II," NSC Contingency Press Guidance. U.S. Internal Memo, August 16, 1995.
[53] "Japanese Biological Warfare Experiments in World War II," NSC Contingency Press Guidance. U.S. Internal Memo, August 16, 1995.
[54] Global Alliance, 27.

Some survivors of the Bataan Death March were believed to have been shipped to facilities like Unit 731 [55]

A former worker at the Mukden camp confirmed in a testimony that American POWs were used as biological warfare test subjects, stating that his group researched dysentery by giving the American subjects "infected materials to drink and carried out autopsies to ascertain the symptoms."[56]

One of the most incriminating pieces of evidence to support the claim that the Japanese experimented on Allied POWs can be inferred from the diary of Mark G.

[55] Digital image. Prisoners of War, 1943. https://www.awm.gov.au/collection/P00761.011

[56] Global Alliance, 27. Testimony of Tsuneji Shimada.

Hearst, an Army captain that was held captive as a prisoner of war in the Mukden Prisoner of War camp. Mark and his fellow American prisoners were given repeated "inoculations" by Japanese doctors in the camp who told them they were simply vaccinations to ward off diseases. Mark recorded the amount of these injections that were given to him and his men in a secret diary that was kept under the mattress of the "sickest man in the camp" whom the Japanese would not risk searching. Below is a excerpt from his diary:

This page clearly shows the many "inoculations" given by the Japanese[57]

___

57 Digital image. 1945. In *The Diary of Mark G*, http://www.mukdenpows.org/Maj%20Herbst%20Documents/Herbst%20Diary.htm.

Hearst's entry shows that he and other POWs were infected with smallpox, typhoid, dysentery, and cholera. However, in the internal memo from 1995, it is stated that the U.S. government, while aware "that former POW's at Mukden received injections, that conditions in the camp were terrible, and that US POW's suffered and died," there is "no conclusive evidence that biological warfare experiments were performed on Americans there."[58] These instances of contradiction in the primary sources regarding Japan's biological warfare are commonplace, which makes research difficult for historians.

Mustard Gas & Toxic Chemicals

Unit 731 collaborated with other facilities in conducting mustard gas experiments, which included the forced ingestion of sulfur mustard. Drinking liquid sulfur mustard resulted in vomiting and diarrhea, and severe eye damage or even blindness in higher doses. Painful blisters would also form on the skin and would become ulcers after bursting when exposed to poison gas.[59]

Unit 731 also researched other deadly chemicals, which included hydrogen cyanide, acetone cyanide, and

[58] "Japanese Biological Warfare Experiments in World War II," NSC Contingency Press Guidance. U.S. Internal Memo, August 16, 1995.
[59] Yamada, 358. Testimony from Witness Furuichi.

potassium cyanide. Hydrogen cyanide was used for bomb research as well as for contaminating enemy water supplies. After ingesting these deadly chemicals, test subjects were unlikely to survive for much longer.[60] One instance of the forced ingestion of toxic materials by subjects was recalled in the Khabarovsk Trials, in which a prisoner was forced to eat porridge laced with a gram of heroin.[61]

Pressure Experiments

Pressure experiments were conducted to research the human body's response to different levels of pressure and how much pressure a body could handle before combustion. Subjects were spun in high-speed centrifuges and placed in pressure chambers, after death, they would be dissected and examined for external and internal damage.

According to the Khabarovsk War Trials, the purpose of the pressure chambers was described as testing "the limits of endurance of the human organism at high altitudes."[62] Done on behalf of the Japanese Air Force[63], test subjects experienced eyes popping out of

---

[60] Global Alliance, 29.
[61] Yamada, 80.
[62] Yamada, 432.
[63] Yamada, 433.

their sockets, blood coming out of their pores, and internal organ damage.[64]

Frostbite Experiments

Frostbite experiments were conducted to find the most effective way to treat Japanese soldiers exposed to the cold in Manchuria and the Soviet Union. Test subjects would be forced to stand outside overnight while barefoot, and sometimes their hands or feet were placed in water and allowed to freeze.[65] Test subjects were not always fully cured of frostbite and sometimes their limbs were amputated. Gangrene was likely to develop in these subjects, and they would die in agony or would be shot once their bodies were no longer useful for research.[66]

Other experiments

In addition to research experiments described above, there were a number of other experiments performed in the name of medical science. Some subjects were hung upside down and timed to see how long it took for them to choke to death. Other subjects had air injected into their blood vessels to study embolisms.[67]

---

[64]Global Alliance, 30.
[65] Yamada, 357-8. Testimony from Witness Furuichi.
[66] Grunden, 190.
[67] Harris, 62.

CHAPTER 5

Deployment of Biological and Chemical Weapons

Germ Warfare and Chemical Warfare

The Japanese Army conducted field experiments to test the efficiency of their biological weapons for use in attacks. The Army found that the most effective method used to infect enemies was deploying fleas taken from infected rats, then dropping them on a population in clay bombs. Another effective method of attack was contaminating water sources with such intestinal diseases as typhus, cholera, and dysentery.

In addition to biological weapons, the Japanese army also used chemical weapons like tear gas, sneezing gas, choking gas, poisonous gas, and rotting gas. Different sizes of bombs and grenades were utilized to deploy these weapons. Chemical bombs were often used by the Japanese when Chinese resistance fighters were particularly fierce. According to the Sanders Report, the Japanese Army created at least eight kinds of special bombs that were utilized for spreading diseases, including bombs that exploded into smaller shrapnel fragments and caused illness and death for the majority of test subjects standing in the field.[68]

It is very difficult to figure out the exact figures and dates when these weapons were utilized due to the lack of evidence available after the war, and therefore, we may never truly know the true extent of their deployment.

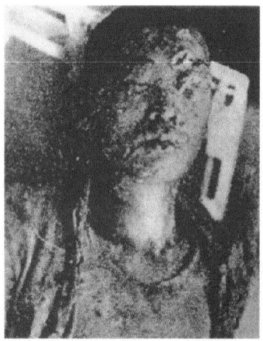

Victim of Japanese chemical weapon[69]

[68] Sanders Report.
[69] Global Alliance, 31.

Germ Warfare in Central China

There were a number of instances in which Unit 731 deployed its research into the field against enemies. What follows are examples of the biological and chemical attacks that took place during the Second Sino-Japanese War, as well as the greater conflict during World War II. The varied locations and enemies these attacks targeted illustrate not only the indiscriminate nature in which the Japanese were willing to use these new weapons, but also how advanced in both technique and foresight the Japanese were able to use them.

Japanese troops with chemical warfare protective gear[70]

---

[70] Global Alliance, 39.

The 1940 bubonic plague attack in Eastern Zhejiang province

In May of 1940, members of Unit 731 loaded a plane with infected fleas on the city of Ningbo in Zhejiang province. These fleas were put into food and water sources, beginning a plague epidemic in that region. While infested fleas rained from the skies above, a train carrying cholera bacteria and typhoid bacteria was brought into the province and its cargo dispersed into the local water supplies. While the members of Unit 731 wanted to kill and inflict misery on the local population, this attack was also used to learn the effects of this type of biological warfare and the possible countermeasures taken by the local population to stem the epidemics.[71]

In October of that same year, a Japanese plane dropped rice and wheat mixed with fleas on the city of Quzhou. This city had no history of bubonic plague, yet over a month after the arrival of the enemy plane, the town was overcome by plague lasting over three weeks and resulting in 21 deaths. It was determined that rats were attracted to the food source that was mixed with fleas, resulting in them spreading throughout the town and causing the epidemic.[72]

---

[71] Barenblatt, 132-133.
[72] Barenblatt, 186.

Bubonic Plague Epidemics in Changde and Beyond

In November of 1941, Unit 731 dropped fleas, wheat, corn, and paper infested with the bubonic plague on the city of Changde in Hunan Province. The plague epidemic began nearly instantaneously, and would lead to at least 7,643 Chinese deaths.[73]

Bubonic plague outbreaks were also recorded in other regions of China where Japanese planes dropped flea bombs, wheat seeds, and other methods of contamination. Outbreaks also occurred in Chu county and Jinhwa county according to Dr. Tsen's testimony, and the existence of the bubonic plague was confirmed in laboratory tests:

"On October 22nd, 1940, a Japanese airplane was circling at a low altitude in the Ningpo area, dropping a large quantity of wheat and cotton. About a week later, Ningpo found its first plague victim, which was confirmed through medical examination. After that, 99 cases were reported and 97 of these people died..."

Dr. Wang Yee Tsen - chief physician of the disease prevention station in Chekiang[74]

---

[73] Barenblatt, 143-144.
[74] Global Alliance, 34.

In addition to Japanese planes infecting civilians in villages from the air, a former soldier claimed that the Army would also "pour germs into the wells and rivers to poison civilians," and would also leave bottles filled with plague-infected fleas by the Chinese army camps.[75]

Cholera Epidemics in Southern China

In 1938 and 1939, Japanese warplanes bombed Yangjian County in Guangdong with plague and cholera-ridden bombs. In addition to bombs, cotton filled with a jelly-like substance was dropped, and it was discovered that the jelly was a breeding ground for bacteria and capable of quickly spreading cholera. Within a year, cholera epidemics broke out across Guangdong and Fujian province, it is estimated that over a million civilians died in that year alone.

The Japanese Army also sent Chinese spies that were disguised as refugees to go behind enemy lines. These spies carried containers filled with cholera, tuberculosis, and dysentery, and covertly poisoned water supplies and food sources.[76] The volunteer spies were sent to sabotage Chinese forces and civilians, and were

---

[75] Testimony of Kozawa, former member of Unit Army 1644 in Nanjing, quoted in Global Alliance, 36.
[76] Global Alliance, 37.

also a part of the attacks against the Soviets, including in the Nomonhan Incident.[77]

The Nomonhan Incident

The Chinese were not the only peoples to suffer from Ishii's biological warfare program. In May 1939, the Japanese and Soviet Union engaged in a full-scale skirmish on the eastern border of the Japanese puppet state of Manchukuo. Ishii took this opportunity to test his biological warfare against the much-despised Soviets.[78] In July, two teams were dispatched to contaminate the sole water source for Manchukuo, the Halha River, with salmonella and typhoid bacteria. Shells packed with containers of bacteria were also used against the Soviets, yet there was inconclusive evidence as to the effectiveness of such weapons. While both Soviet and Japanese soldiers did experience plague, dysentery, and cholera, it is indiscernible whether this was caused by Japan's biological weapons, or the geography of the area in which this conflict was fought.[79]

---

[77] Harris, 61.
[78] Japan joined Nazi Germany in the Anti-Comintern Pact in 1936. Fascist Italy would soon follow, creating a global alliance against the Soviet Union.
[79] Harris, 74-76.

Japanese troops undergoing chemical warfare training[80]

Cherry Blossoms at Night: The Planned U.S. Attack

One of the most interesting (and far-fetched) plans for the use of biological warfare by the Japanese was an attack on the American mainland in the city of San Diego, California. Dubbed "Cherry Blossoms at Night," the plan called for the Japanese to send a plane-carrying submarine to the California coast, send that plane to San Diego, and release bacteria-infected fleas on the city. Ishii began planning and recruiting for this mission

---

[80] Global Alliance, 31.

upon its approval in March of 1945.[81] The scheduled date for this attack was September 22nd, 1945. However, the attack was ultimately called off by General Yoshijiro Umezu in its final planning stages. Umezu understood that the plan served no military purpose and would only embolden the United States to defeat its rival in the Pacific. The Japanese were more concerned with using their war materiel to protect the Japanese mainland, which by this point was under constant bombardment. The dropping of the atomic bombs on Hiroshima and Nagasaki on August 6th and August 9th, respectively, and the resultant unconditional surrender of Japan, cancelled the ongoing debate of this operation.[82]

---

[81] Barenblatt, 189-190.

[82] "Operation Cherry Blossom at Night" from *weaponsandwarfare.com*, May 12, 2015

CHAPTER 6

The Fall

Destruction of Evidence

On August 8th, 1945, the day after the atomic bombing of Hiroshima and Nagasaki, the Soviet Union formally declared war on Imperial Japan, launching an invasion into North East China and Korea. At this point in the war, the Japanese army had been depleted and could not manage a strong defence against the Soviets. Fearful that their research would fall into the hands of the Soviets, the officers at Unit 731 ordered that every trace of Unit 731, and the rest of the related facilities, be destroyed by dynamite.[83] Buildings were demolished, testing equipments destroyed, and files burned. Any of the prisoners who had not yet been killed in experiments were "killed, cremated, and cast into the Songhuajiang River" outside of Harbin.[84]

---

[83] "Unmasking horror: A special report."
[84] Tsuchiya.

This systematic destruction of potentially incriminating evidence occurred throughout the empire following the surrender of the Japanese. A professor at Japan's National Defense Academy estimated that of all the Japanese Army and Navy documents that existed during the war, maybe less than 0.1 percent survived the purge.[85]

After much of the evidence was destroyed, the infected rats and fleas were released en mass to the surrounding countryside, which caused an estimated 20,000-30,000 deaths.[86] A chief of a branch of Unit 731 also ordered that his officers were given cyanide pills to poison themselves with, in case they were captured and forced to confess their crimes. This chief of the branch was one of the officers interrogated for the Khabarovsk Trials, and he admitted that he was "fully aware of Ishii's plans" during the facility's lifetime.[87]

In the Thompson Report, something of interest is mentioned in the conclusion. Thompson notes that all of the sources who were interrogated regarding biological warfare were consistent with one another, which insinuates that "the informants had been

---

[85] Tanaka, Hiromi. *A catalog of captured former army and navy materials at the Library of Congress.* Tokyo: Toyo shorin, 1995. Quoted in Drea, et al, 26.
[86] "Japanese veteran admits vivisection on PoWs;" Bix, 687.
[87] Testimony of Nishi. Yamada, 458.

instructed as to the amount and nature of information that was to be divulged under interrogation."[88] Again, as the majority of the written documents and physical evidence, such as dead bodies and buildings, were destroyed, oral testimonies have been a large part of the evidence condemning the Japanese army for their facilitation of biological warfare research.

Ruins of 731 after the Japanese withdrawal[89]

---

[88] Thompson Report.
[89] Burned out Unit 731 facility. Digital Image. Historical Firearms. 2011 http://www.historicalfirearms.info/post/101447057369/real-horror-japanese-human-experimentation-during

CHAPTER 7

Post-War "Legacy"

Remnants of Japanese Chemical Bombs

While it has been over 70 years since the war ended, the germs developed by the Japanese continue to pose a threat to whole communities in areas where germ warfare was utilized. In addition to this, the Japanese also left behind huge quantities of chemical bombs, which are still being discovered to this day. In a treaty signed by China and Japan in 2003, Japan promised to help excavate and safely remove the unexploded chemical bombs. The Vice President of the Heilongjiang Academy of Social Sciences estimated in 2004 that the Japanese Army left behind 2 million unexploded chemical bombs throughout dozens of Chinese villages and provinces after the Japanese defeat in 1945.[90]

When these bombs were discovered after the war, the Chinese lacked the resources to dispose of them,

---

[90] "Chinese, Japanese Experts Clear some 540 Unexploded Bombs in Northeast China." *BBC Monitoring Asia Pacific*, June 24, 2004.

and consequently, many were buried underground and largely forgotten. Because these munitions have been buried for so long, the metallic cases of the bombs have rusted, making it difficult to safely remove these bombs by any mechanical means. The damage to the bombs also means that chemicals have leaked into the soil, causing great damage to the surrounding environment.

Even today, the process to safely dispose of these munitions is long and demanding. As China continues to develop its economy, and cities continue to expand, these buried munitions cause great harm to unfortunate laborers that unknowingly unearth them. Most notable was the disaster at Qiqihar City, where construction workers uncovered a metal drum and unwittingly opened it. The drum was filled with mustard gas, and 34 people were sent to the hospital. There was one fatality, and all of those who came into contact with the gas experienced symptoms such as headaches, difficulty breathing, and sores.[91]

---

[91] "Gas Bomb Cleanup Continues," *China Daily*, September 13, 2003.

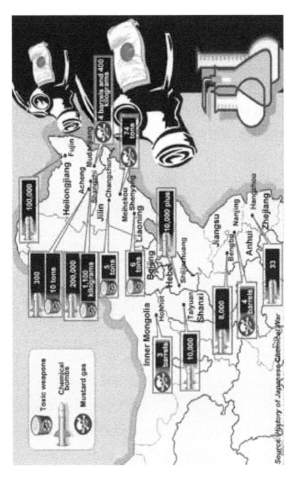

Map of discovered chemical weapons remnants[92]

---

[92] Digital Image from "Gas Bomb Cleanup Continues,"
http://www.chinadaily.com.cn/en/doc/2003-
09/13/content_263776.htm

59

"Decaying Leg Villages": Living Evidence

While it has been more than 70 years since Japan's defeat in WWII, the bioweapons deployed during the war continue to cause suffering and pain among the Chinese population. Most notable of this is the existence of what locals call "Decaying Leg disease" in the areas where germ weapons were deployed.

The "decaying leg" disease is characterized by the development of raw, festering wounds on the legs, these wounds rarely heal, and the victims are always at risk of secondary infections. Victims of the disease often endure great suffering from their wounds, and are forced to live sheltered lives.

In March 2002, a team of academics from U.S. and Chinese universities concluded that these "decaying leg" cases were linked to the Japanese deployment of biological weapons, as they exhibited symptoms that were a combination of both anthrax and glanders, something which had not existed in China before the war.[93]

---

[93] Li, Xiaofang, *Blood-Weeping Accusations: Records of Anthrax Victims* (China: Central Literature Publishing House, 2005), 4.

A victim of the "decaying leg" disease[94]

Testimonies from Victims

In his work, *Blood-Weeping Accusations*, Li Xiaofang returns to a number of villages that were invaded by the Japanese in the Pacific Theater during World War II to document the lingering effects of chemical and biological warfare used by the Japanese in China. For four years, Li recorded the recollections of survivors of the Japanese invasion, many of whom continued to

---

[94] Japan's Biological and Chemical Warfare in China during WWII. Digital Image. Don Tow's website, 2009.
http://dontow.com/photos/Ruan_Shufeng.jpg

suffer from lesions and other infections that had a tremendous impact on their daily lives. These testimonies present a connection between the coming of the Japanese Army and the occurrence of skin lesions and other infections, some of which came to have a major impact on the daily lives of Chinese villagers in the region.

Survivors of these attacks were performing daily routines and duties when the effects of the chemical and biological warfare deployed by the Japanese began to have an impact on their daily lives. Hua Qing-yun (1922-2002) of Jinhua City talked of him and his father cutting firewood in the mountains when an itching blister appeared on his leg. Xie Zhangshi of Naoqiao Village remembered performing farm work and washing his hands in a ditch alongside a road. After obtaining a cut on his foot, he developed an ulcer that burned, swelled, and eventually resulted in the loss of two toes. All of these testimonies stem from the time period of the Japanese invasion of the region in the early 1940s. Chinese citizens consistently refer to the invading forces as "Japanese devils," and talk of bodies floating in water, decapitations, and the horrid treatment of women at the hands of the invading Japanese army. The following quotes from *Blood-Weeping Accusations* encapsulate the treatment the Japanese inflicted on these rural villagers,

the biological warfare employed on these people, and the
effects of those weapons:

Hua Qing-yun (1922-2002), Jinhua City, Zhejiang (PAGE 51)

"One day in September 1942, my father and I were cutting firewood in the mountain when an itching blister appeared on my leg. Thinking it was caused by the scratch of branches, I didn't care about it. My leg suddenly turned red and swollen in the evening. Then it began to ulcerate and the fester flesh kept falling one piece after another. My father's leg also ulcerated. At that time, over 20 villagers were infected by ulcerative skin lesions on legs. My father died of it five years later. My family was too poor to have money to cure it. My mother picked herbs to

63

treat my legs but they didn't work. When I was 17, the ulceration was so serious that I was unable to work. My mother had to support the family alone. Over a decade ago, my mother passed away and nobody took care of my life. I have to spend the rest of my life with the minimum allowance of 2 yuan per day given by the Government and alms given by my neighbours. Several days ago, the lower part of my leg disjointed due to the ulceration. Now I cannot stand up. I just sit here and wait for the end of my life."

 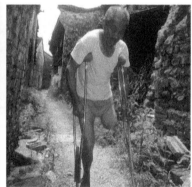

Zhang Bing-tao, (1920-), Jinhua City, Zhejiang

"When I was 23 years old, in August 1942, shortly after Japanese devils left our village, over 30 residents in our village were infected by ulcerative skin lesions on legs.

And a lot of livestock died. My uncle and elder brother both died of the ulcerated legs. One bone was taken from my leg. After 1949, my ulcerated leg was cured with penicillin. Now my legs cannot walk normally I have to walk with the walking stick."

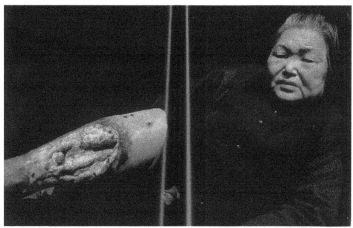

Yang Chun-lian (1920-2003), Longyou County, Zhejiang

"60 years ago, in June 1942, when I was still a child, Japanese devils invaded our village. They shit and urinated in villagers' rice jars, and raped. I saw them shoot villagers. Fortunately, having known about their crimes, my family cut my hair short and dressed me up like a boy. Three little friends and I escaped from the village stealthily. On our way, I stepped on several corpses. Many corpses were floating on the ponds and brooks.

Shortly after the retreat of Japanese Devils, many villagers developed ulcerative skin lesions on their legs. My right leg also blistered, red, swollen and itching. I vomited and had a high fever. Later my leg began to ulcerate. The ulceration was so serious that the artery broke and blood gushed out like a spring. My life was saved in time. But I'm unable to walk now.

Zheng Xiang-jin, (1916-2003), Shangrao County, Jiangxi

"In June 1942, Japanese devils invaded our village. They burnt almost all the houses. My uncle's head was chopped down by a Japanese devil with his sword. The head rolled

66

on the ground, his eyes still winking. His mouth was open, trying to say some words but failed. The blood from his body ejected far away. They raped every woman they had seen. One woman's genitals were ripped off after they had raped her. And old woman who ran slowly was caught by a japanese devil, he shot her in the head. Their brutality made us tremble: some of us fainted on the ground. That September, many friends and my legs blistered and ulcerated. The wounds were as black as charcoal. I believe it must be caused by Japanese devils' germs."

Instances such as this demonstrate the invasive nature of biological weaponry on the local population when it was deployed. Whether permeating a roadside ditch or making its way up to a mountain farm, Japanese biological weapons were manufactured in such a way as to promote what Ishii and Unit 731 were hoping to achieve, a new type of weapon that could wreak havoc on a civilian population. Not only did people become sick or disabled from the use of chemical and biological weapons; Chinese citizens continued to live with "rotten leg syndrome" and other ulcerated limbs well into the 21st Century.

CHAPTER 8

Post-War Denial

Imperial Contradictions

It can be difficult to confirm whether the emperor of Japan, Hirohito, was complicit or even aware of the Japanese Army's research in bacteriological warfare. Following the death of Hirohito in 1989, "debate has raged over the extent to which [the Emperor] was culpable for Japan's wartime past, with some critics claiming he was complicit in the atrocities," while others claim he disagreed with the Army's aggression.[95] Even today it is still relatively taboo to speak ill of the Emperor, as he was "the nation's highest spiritual authority."[96] During the Khabarovsk Trials, an attorney of a man on trial pointed out that there was a systematic indoctrination in the Army of the spiritual nature of the emperor. He claimed that men like his client were

---

[95] "Declassified British document depicts Emperor Hirohito as being wary of WWII military aggression." *Japan Times*, July 20, 2017.
[96] Bix, 16.

"stuffed with sundry mythology" about how the Emperor was descended from the sun goddess and that his divine family "had to be obeyed blindly and unquestioningly."[97]

While any army directives "were as a rule shown to the emperor," this is difficult to prove because "no extant documents directly link [Hirohito] to bacteriological warfare."[98] In a document written for an American colonel, a Japanese doctor insisted that the Emperor was not pleased with "the preparation of chemical warfare in the Japanese Army," and that the bacteriological research was explained by the government as "purely defensive."

Dr. Naito refuted the government statement as false but maintained that Hirohito was not involved. He even confirmed that pathogens such as the plague, cholera, dysentery, and anthrax were studied and tested.[99] In the report to the American colonel that Dr. Naito had written to, Sanders states again that the biological warfare research "was apparently done

---

[97] Yamada, 474. Speech by Counsel Belov, N.P., in defense of Accused Yamada.
[98] Bix, Herbert P. *Hirohito and the Making of Modern Japan*. New York: HarperCollins, 2000. 362-4.
[99] Naito, Ryoichi. "The Naito Document: Private (Secret) Information to Colonel Sanders." 1945. Printed in Williams & Wallace.

without the knowledge (and possibly contrary to the wishes) of the Emperor."[100] Additionally, in the Inglis Report, it is noted that there were "personal objections of the Emperor" in regards to biological warfare research, but there was "no further evidence or comment made on this point."[101]

In one of the Khabarovsk trial transcripts conducted by the Soviets, a former Unit 731 colonel said that he saw the secret decree that Hirohito issued to create Unit 731 in 1936. Kawashima confirms that there was research on epidemic prevention in the 1930s, and that there was also the sanctioning of offensive research. He saw another one of the emperor's secret decrees in 1940 that added 3,000 workers to the Pingfan facility and officially initiated the new focus on bacteriological warfare. Kawashima also confirmed that he was aware that Ishii conducted bacteriological research in Manchuria as early as 1932.[102]

In addition to the emperor, other high officials were aware and involved in Ishii's endeavors. The Chief of Military Affairs Division of the Army Ministry, Major

---

[100] Sanders. "The Sanders Report: Report on Scientific Intelligence Survey in Japan, September - October 1945." 1945. Printed in Williams & Wallace.

[101] Inglis, Thomas B. "The Inglis Report: Naval aspects biological warfare." August 1947. Printed in Williams & Wallace.

[102] Yamada, 112, 114. Testimony from Kiyoshi Kawashima.

General Nagata, gave 200,000 yen to Ishii's research program in 1934.[103] And in 1941, the Chief of the General Japanese Staff urged in an order that the unit must "[speed up the] research work on plague bacteria as a means of bacteriological warfare."[104] Additionally, from 1937-1945, Ishii received an annual budget of 6 million yen from the Japanese Army.[105]

Governmental Contradictions

In 1984, Professor Takao Matsumura and some of his students from Keio University were in a Tokyo bookstore researching World War II when they stumbled upon a cache of primary documents. These papers written by Japanese military officers, in September 1945, had evidence confirming that Unit 731 performed experiments on Chinese prisoners. There was also evidence that American officials occupying Japan discussed obtaining the research that Unit 731 amassed during its operation.[106]

However, this exchange of information for immunity has been a point of contention amongst

---

[103] Grunden, 187.
[104] Yamada, 113. Testimony from Kawashima.
[105] Grunden, 193.
[106] Tyson, James. "Proof found of Japanese gas, germ tests on POWs." *United Press International*, August 16, 1984.

historians. In some historical scholarship, there are allegations that there was a secret plea bargain that the United States brokered with Ishii to exchange medical research for immunity from war crime prosecution. In a letter written in 1998, the Director of the Department of Justice's Office of Special Investigations in Los Angeles confirmed that the exchange occurred:

"Two of these [formerly classified] reports [about biological warfare data collected by the Japanese and the arrangement made between the United States and Lieutenant General Shiro Ishii, the Commander of the Unit 731], dated November 17th, 1981 and May 5th, 1982, confirm that Ishii and his colleagues received immunity from prosecution and that, in exchange, they provided a great deal of information to U.S. authorities." [107]

In contrast, in an internal memo written in 1995 by Edward Drea, then the Chief of the Research and Analysis Division of Military History, Drea claims that "there is no primary source material guaranteeing General Ishii immunity from prosecution. He was not tried as a war criminal apparently in order to conceal from the Soviet Union the extent of the information he

---

[107] Letter, December 17, 1998. Headed "Re: U.S. Non-prosecution of Japanese War Criminals," sent to the associate dean of the Simon Wiesenthal Center, Los Angeles. Quoted in Reynolds, 22.

73

provided the United States about biological warfare. Even that interpretation, however, rests on very fragmentary evidence."[108]

Another primary government source, an internal memo, admits that with the emergence of the Cold War, the Americans felt that they could not release the Japanese research to the world because the Soviets would have access to the sensitive information. Thus, the documents that the Japanese gave to the Americans were classified and were unable to be used in the Tokyo War Crimes Trials. This same source also states, when asked directly about whether Ishii was granted immunity in exchange for information, that they "have been unable to locate conclusive evidence that such a deal was made."[109]

Additionally, in another government source from 10 years prior, in 1985, there is an excerpt that states something different:

---

[108] Drea, Edward. "Memorandum for the Undersecretary of the Army: Information on WWI POWs." Department of the Army Center for Military History, May 10, 1995. Quoted in Cunliffe, William H. "Nazi War Crimes and Japanese Imperial Government Records: Select Documents on Japanese War Crimes and Japanese Biological Warfare, 1934-2006." Interagency Working Group, 5.
[109] "Japanese Biological Warfare Experiments in World War II," NSC Contingency Press Guidance. U.S. Internal Memo, August 16, 1995.

"What was the background of the agreement between MacArthur and the Japanese scientists?"

"The agreement...was done at the recommendation of intelligence personnel and B/W [biological warfare] experts who were part of the State, War, and Navy Coordinating Committee. The Japanese would not discuss their experimentation and the Americans threatened to turn them over to the Russians. The Japanese then agreed to talk if they were not prosecuted. The Committee wanted all information gathered to be kept in-house. This subject was a national security concern at that time."[110]

It is clear in this source, as well as in others, that the value of the biological warfare research was "of such importance to national security as to far outweigh the value accruing from war crimes prosecution."[111]

Japanese Government's Stance

One of the arguments made by the Japanese who defend Unit 731's work is that their work was purely defensive, but in a testimony from the Chief of the Medical

---

[110] Oland, Dwight. "Source Search for Primary Material on Japanese Biological Warfare." Memo to Dr. Schieps, from the U.S. Department of the Army Chief of Military History. December 16, 1985.
[111] State-War-Navy Coordinating Subcommittee for the Far East, September 1947. Quoted in Grunden, 196.

Administration of the Army, he confessed that the type of bacterial culture that Ishii cultivated meant that "these bacteria could not be used for the preparation of vaccines, and could only be used for the mass production of microbes for use in bacteriological warfare."[112]

Since the end of World War II, the Japanese government has made several apologies for its behavior during the war, however, they typically avoid mentioning specific facts and atrocities, to the anger of many.[113] Various statesmen over the years have apologized for the pain and damage that Japan caused, but other Asian countries feel that there has never been a "full, direct, unambiguous apology" for all of the atrocities that were committed.[114] Despite the cover-up by Japanese and American governments, the Japanese government "has repeatedly apologized for its part in the war and acknowledges that it caused tremendous damage and suffering. But it has never officially recognized the atrocities that took place at Unit 731."[115]

---

[112] Yamada, 305. Testimony from Kajitsuka, Chief of the Medical Administration of the Kwantung Army Headquarters.
[113] "South Korea Urges Japan to Reflect on Wartime Chemical Warfare Unit." *BBC Monitoring International Reports*, 2013.
[114] Reynolds, 19.
[115] Connor, Neil. "70 Years On, Unit 731's wartime atrocities fester in China's memory." *Japan Times*, February 12, 2015.

The current Prime Minister of Japan, Shinzo Abe, heads what has been called a "myopic and exonerating revisionist narrative of history." His "vague and ambiguous references to past misdeeds" fail to adequately "[recognize] Japanese aggression and the horrors inflicted" with "minimalist nods toward contrition."[116] Because of the Japanese government's continued lack of a full apology of their war crimes, Asian countries continue to wait for official recognition that is more than 70 years late.

Textbooks and Education

In the 1980s, the Japanese government came under fire for alleged attempts to "tone down descriptions of Japanese aggression" in government-issued textbooks for middle schoolers.[117] At that time, the Ministry of Education "stated that there was still no reliable research concerning Unit 731, so it was still too early to raise this issue in textbooks."[118]

However, in a series of lawsuits filed for 30 years by Saburo Ienaga, an education professor, the court ruled in 1997 that the Ministry of Education had gone

---

[116] Kingston, Jeff. "Abe's revisionism and Japan's divided war memories." *Japan Times*, August 22, 2015.
[117] Drea, et al. 26.
[118] Statement of the Ministry of Education, 1983. Quoted in Global Alliance, 49.

too far in censoring history textbooks. One issue of import was the usage of the term "military advancement" rather than "aggression." Specifically, in regards to Unit 731, the Ministry of Education's statement that there was not enough reliable research was refuted. The ministry had demanded that all references of Unit 731 be taken out of textbooks, but the court ruled that "the atrocities of Unit 731 had been established beyond denial" based on first-person confessions and testimonies from people who participated in or witnessed human experiments.[119]

In 2000, a textbook revisionist movement headed by the Japanese Society for History Textbook Reform was started with Fujioka Nobukatsu, a professor of education at Tokyo University. He started his conservative history curriculum reform in the 1990s, and said he wanted to "correct history by emphasizing a positive view of Japan's past and remove from textbooks any reference to matters associated with…'dark history' issues…that might make Japanese schoolchildren uncomfortable when they read about the Pacific War."[120]

---

[119] Kristof, Nicholas D. "Japan Bars Censorship of Atrocities." *New York Times*, August 30, 1997.
[120] Masalski, Kathleen Woods. "Examining the Japanese History Textbook Controversies." *Japan Digest*, November 2001.

CONCLUSION

Justice

Despite some coverup of Japan's biological warfare program, the Soviet Union tried twelve officials in the Khabarovsk military tribunal in 1949.[121] In Khabarovsk, a former Unit 100 worker confirmed that he had "taken part in these inhuman experiments on living people, in bacteriological sabotage and in the preparations for bacteriological warfare against the Soviet Union."[122]

Unfortunately, the United States "dismissed the verdicts [in the Khabarovsk trials] with the evidence as another in a series of long-running Stalinist show trials."[123] The U.S. denied the truth uncovered from these trials, despite the argument that they were well aware of, and had been for years, "of what the Japanese on trial were saying...pieced together from their own

---

[121] *The Story of Unit 731*, 47.

[122] Yamada, 325.

[123] Drea, Edward et al. *Researching Japanese War Crimes: Introductory Essays.* Washington, D.C.: Nazi War Crimes and Japanese Imperial Government Records Interagency Working Group, 2006. 7.

intelligence officers, assembled from the stories of prisoners of war and civilian internees, and confirmed by members of Unit 731 and 100 who had fallen into their hands" after the conclusion of World War II.[124]

In the Khabarovsk trials, which tried 12 Japanese officials that were a part of Ishii's biological warfare research conglomeration, the 12 men received prison sentences that ranged from 2-25 years. Most were freed less than 15 years later, which is in severe contrast with the war crime trials held in Nuremburg and Tokyo: in these trials, some German and Japanese officials received sentences of life in prison or were hanged.[125]

A number of the medical doctors that served in Unit 731 went on to long, prominent careers in post-war Japan, unlike their Nazi counterparts during the Nuremberg Trials. Some former members went on to become directors of medical institutions and universities. They were also placed on the 1964 Olympic Committee, posted as the head of the Green Cross, and were members of the National Institute of Health.[126]

---

[124] Williams & Wallace, 231.

[125] Working, Russell. "The trial of Unit 731." *Japan Times*, June 5, 2001.

[126] Devolder, Katrien. "U.S. Complicity and Japan's Wartime Medical Atrocities: Time for a Response." *The American Journal of Bioethics*, 15(6): 40-49, 2015.

Although Ishii demanded that his former workers take an oath of secrecy, there were investigations undertaken in 1945 by the United States. In a report written in 1945 following the Japanese surrender, Thompson concluded that it was "evident throughout the interrogations that it was the desire of the Japanese to minimize the extent of their activities in biological warfare, especially the effort devoted to offensive research and development."[127] However, as some of the testimonies throughout this book have shown, including those from the Khabarovsk Trials as well as admissions of guilt from the 1980s, the creation of vaccines and other defensive bacteriological experiments were just the tip of the iceberg.

The contradictions in the historical scholarship, including sources that argue whether the Emperor was aware of Unit 731's existence and sources that argue whether there was a plea bargain between Ishii and the U.S., make it clear that this topic still needs work. The lack of sources from the Japanese are a result of the destruction of incriminating evidence, but there are oral testimonies that can serve as evidence. There are sources that can be found elsewhere, but the problem is still that these sources are scattered.

---

[127] Thompson Report.

While it has been a long time since the destruction of Unit 731, it still continues to cause suffering among the Chinese people today. The chemical and gas bombs left behind continue to poison the natural environment and cause great pain to anyone unfortunate enough to discover them. Any remaining victims of the decaying leg disease continue to live out their lives in relative obscurity.

Little is known about Japan's secret biological weapons program due to the cover up by both the Japanese and American governments. Few people today know about these crimes, and the majority of the perpetrators were never prosecuted for the deaths of an unknown number of civilians.

There can be no peace for the survivors and victims until full acknowledgement of these crimes are known throughout the world.

REFERENCES

Secondary Sources

Barenblatt, Daniel. *A Plague Upon Humanity: The Secret Genocide of Axis Japan's Germ Warfare Operation.* New York: HarperCollins, 2004.

Bix, Herbert P. *Hirohito and the Making of Modern Japan.* New York: HarperCollins, 2000. 362-4.

Byrd, Gregory Dean "General Ishii Shiro: His Legacy is That of Genius and Madman." Masters Thesis, East Tennessee State University, 2005.

Chauhan, Sharad. 2014. *Biological Weapon.* New Dehli: APH Publishing.

Devolder, Katrien. "U.S. Complicity and Japan's Wartime Medical Atrocities: Time for a Response." *The American Journal of Bioethics,* 15(6): 40-49, 2015.

Drea, Edward; Bradsher, Greg; Hanyok, Robert; Lide, James; Petersen, Michael, & Daqing Yang. *Researching Japanese War Crimes: Introductory Essays.* Washington, D.C.: Nazi War Crimes and

Japanese Imperial Government Records Interagency Working Group, 2006.

Federation of American Scientists. "Biological Weapons Program." 2000. Accessed via Alpha Education online resources.

Global Alliance for Preserving the History of WWII in Asia. 2008. *The Story of Unit 731.* Global Alliance .

Grunden, Walter E. *Secret weapons and World War II: Japan in the shadow of big science.* Lawrence, Kansas: University Press of Kansas, 2005.

Harris, Sheldon. *Factories of Death: Japanese Biological Warfare, 1932-45, and the American Cover-up.* New York: Routledge Press, 1994.

Pawlowicz, Rachel and Grunden, Walter. "Teaching Atrocities: The Holocaust and Unit 731 in Secondary School Curriculum." *History Teacher*, Vol. 48 Issue 2, p. 271-294. February 2015.

Rees, Laurence. *Horror in the East: Japan and the Atrocities of World War II.* London: Da Capo Press, 2001.

Tow, Don. "Japan's Biological and Chemical Warfare in China during WWII." *Don Tow's Website.* April, 2009. http://www.dontow.com/2009/04/japans-biological-and-chemical-warfare-in-china-during-wwii/.

Tsuchiya, Takashi. "The Imperial Japanese Medical Atrocities and its Enduring Legacy in Japanese Research Ethics." Abridged from chapter "The Imperial Japanese Experiments in China" in *Oxford Textbook of Clinical Research Ethics*, 2008.

Unit 731: Japan's biological force. 2008. Directed by BBC.

Watts, Jonathan. "Victims of Japan's notorious Unit 731 sue." *The Lancet*, Vol. 360, p.628. August 24, 2002.

Wilk, Beata Marzana. "The Japanese Biological and Chemical Warfare Program in China, 1932-1945." New Jersey: Masters Thesis, Seton Hall University, 2004.

Williams, Peter & Wallace, David. *Unit 731: Japan's Secret Biological Warfare in World War II.* New York: The Free Press, 1989.

Primary Sources

"Burned out Unit 731 facility." *Historical Firearms.*2011. http://www.historicalfirearms.info/post/1014470573 69/real-horror-japanese-human-experimentation-during .

"Chinese, Japanese Experts Clear some 540 Unexploded Bombs in Northeast China." *BBC Monitoring Asia Pacific*, June 24, 2004.

Connor, Neil. "70 Years On, Unit 731's wartime atrocities fester in China's memory." *Japan Times,* February 12, 2015.

Cunliffe, William H. "Nazi War Crimes and Japanese Imperial Government Records: Select Documents on Japanese War Crimes and Japanese Biological Warfare, 1934-2006." Interagency Working Group.

"Declassified British document depicts Emperor Hirohito as being wary of WWII military aggression." *Japan Times,* July 20, 2017.

"Four prisoners of war (POWs) with beri beri." Australian War Memorial, 1943. https://www.awm.gov.au/collection/P00761.011

"Gas Bomb Cleanup Continues." *China Daily News.* September 13, 2003. http://www.chinadaily.com.cn/en/doc/2003-09/13/content_263776.htm .

Gold, Hal. *Unit 731: Testimony.* 2004.

Herbst, Mark G. 1945. "Diary of Mark G. Herbst." *Mukden Prisoner Of War Remembrance Society.* http://www.mukdenpows.org/Maj%20Herbst%20Documents/Herbst%20Diary.htm.

Inglis, Thomas B. "The Inglis Report: Naval aspects biological warfare." August 1947. Printed in Williams & Wallace.

"Japanese Biological Warfare Experiments in World War II," NSC Contingency Press Guidance. U.S. Internal Memo, August 16, 1995.

"Japanese Special Naval Landing Forces with gas masks and rubber gloves during a chemical attack, Battle of Shanghai, 1937." *Rare Historical Photos.* http://rarehistoricalphotos.com/japanese-special-naval-landing-forces-gas-masks-rubber-gloves-chemical-attack-battle-shanghai-1937/.

Kingston, Jeff. "Abe's revisionism and Japan's divided war memories." *Japan Times*, August 22, 2015.

Kristof, Nicholas D. "Japan Bars Censorship of Atrocities." *New York Times*, August 30, 1997.

Kristoff, Nicholas. "Unmasking Horror -- A special report,: Japan Confronting Gruesome War Atrocity." *New York Times*, March 17, 1995.

Letter, December 17, 1998. Headed "Re: U.S. Non-prosecution of Japanese War Criminals," sent to the associate dean of the Simon Wiesenthal Center, Los Angeles. [Quoted in Reynolds].

Li, Xiaofang. *Blood-Weeping Accusations: Records of Anthrax Victims.* China: Central Literature Publishing House, 2005.

Masalski, Kathleen Woods. "Examining the Japanese History Textbook Controversies." *Japan Digest*, November 2001.

McCurry, Justin. "Japanese veteran admits vivisection tests on Pows." *The Guardian*, November 27, 2006.

Naito, Ryoichi. "The Naito Document: Private (Secret) Information to Colonel Sanders." 1945. Printed in Williams & Wallace.

Oland, Dwight. "Source Search for Primary Material on Japanese Biological Warfare." Memo to Dr. Schieps, from the U.S. Department of the Army Chief of Military History. December 16, 1985.

Parry, Richard Lloyd. "Gruesome secret threatens to surface from city park." *The Times*, January 14, 2011.

Reynolds, Gary. "U.S. Prisoners of War and Civilian American Citizens Captured and Interned by Japan in World War II: The Issue of Compensation." Congressional Research Service Report for Congress, The Library of Congress. Updated 2002.

Sanders. "The Sanders Report: Report on Scientific Intelligence Survey in Japan, September - October 1945." 1945. Printed in Williams & Wallace.

"South Korea Urges Japan to Reflect on Wartime Chemical Warfare Unit." *BBC Monitoring International Reports*, (2013).

Talamadge, Eric. 2004. "Japanese Soldier Faces the Poison of His Past." *Los Angeles Times*, September 19.

Thompson. "The Thompson Report." 1945. Printed in Williams & Wallace

Tyson, James. "Proof found of Japanese gas, germ tests on POWs." *United Press International,* August 16, 1984.

Working, Russell. "The trial of Unit 731." *Japan Times,* June 5, 2001.

Yamada, Otozo. *Materials on the trial of former servicemen of the Japanese Army, charged with manufacturing and employing bacteriological weapon.* Moscow: Foreign Languages Pub. House, 1950. Accessed via Google Books.